BALLOONS

MORE SCIENCE FUN FROM BERNIE ZUBROWSKI, THE BOSTON CHILDREN'S MUSEUM, AND BEECH TREE BOOKS

Blinkers and Buzzers: Building and Experimenting with Electricity and Magnetism

Clocks: Building and Experimenting with Model Timepieces

Mirrors: Finding Out About the Properties of Light

Raceways: Having Fun with Balls and Tracks

Tops: Building and Experimenting with Spinning Toys

Wheels at Work: Building and Experimenting with Models of Machines

BALLOONS

Building and Experimenting with Inflatable Toys

BY BERNIE ZUBROWSKI

ILLUSTRATED BY ROY DOTY

A Boston Children's Museum Activity Book

BEECH TREE BOOKS
New York

Acknowledgments

Thanks to Patti Quinn, who helped me put the final manuscript into a clear and coherent form.

Text copyright © 1990 by Bernard Zubrowski and The Children's Museum, Boston
Illustrations copyright © 1990 by Roy Doty
All rights reserved.
No part of this book may be reproduced
or utilized in any form
or by any means, electronic
or mechanical, including photocopying,
recording or by any information storage
and retrieval system,
without permission in writing from the Publisher.
Inquiries should be addressed to
William Morrow and Company, Inc.,
1350 Avenue of the Americas,
New York, NY 10019

First Beech Tree Edition, 1992.

Printed in the United States of America.
2 3 4 5 6 7 8 9 10

Library of Congress Cataloging-in-Publication Data
Zubrowski, Bernie.
Balloons: building and experimenting with inflatable toys / by
Bernie Zubrowski; illustrated by Roy Doty.
p. cm.—(A Boston Children's Museum activity book)
Summary: Text and experiments introduce scientific principles that
can be demonstrated with balloons and other inflatable toys.
ISBN 0-688-08324-2
1. Balloons—Experiments—Juvenile literature.   2. Science—
Experiments—Juvenile literature.   3. Force and energy—
Experiments—Juvenile literature.   4. Pressure—Experiments—
Juvenile literature.   [1. Balloons—Experiments.   2. Science—
Experiments.   3. Experiments.]   I. Doty, Roy, 1922-   ill.
II. Title.   III. Series.
QC33.Z83   1990
507.8—dc20   89-37265   CIP   AC

To the fifth-graders of the Farragut School of Boston, who were great experimenters with balloons and other projects during the school year of 1986.

CONTENTS

INTRODUCTION

Most people think of balloons only as colorful party decorations. But you can do a lot more with balloons than just look at them. Balloons can be used for toys and games, as well. Fat, round balloons can be rolled and punched. Long, narrow ones can be twisted into all kinds of animal shapes and interesting sculptures. On a hot summer day, you and your friends can cool off with water-filled "bombs."

But that's not all you can do with balloons. You can combine the fun of fooling around with balloons and the challenge of carrying out scientific experiments. Certain properties of balloons allow you to make toys that are easy to assemble *and* fascinating to experiment with. For instance, if you let go of an inflated, untied balloon, air will come rushing out of the neck. The balloon will fly all around the room, darting here and there. You can take advantage of this property to make balloon-propelled

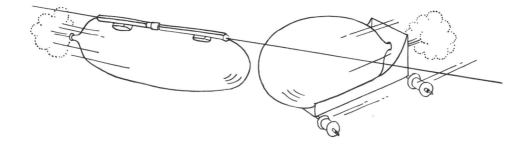

models of cars, boats, and rockets. Then you can experiment to see how fast and how far you can make your models travel.

The projects in this book all use simple, inexpensive, and easily obtainable materials. This was done to encourage you to try as many different experiments as possible. There is a special challenge in using simple materials. It can be very satisfying to see how much you can accomplish with basic items you may already have around your home or classroom.

As you design and construct the models in this book, you will begin to discover some important ideas related to science and engineering. The simple experiments you perform will help you understand some of the physical properties of gases and the scientific concepts of force and pressure.

Some projects will be easy to do, while others may not work so well the first time. Don't give up. Try again. In the process of trying to figure out what went wrong, you will also learn something.

The directions in this book are only one way of making the models. You may come up with better ways of doing things. As you try to improve your models, you may even invent something new! Be patient and persistent; the results you obtain will be worth the effort.

HOW TO BLOW UP A BALLOON

Part of the fun and challenge of playing with balloons is attempting to blow them up without breaking them. You can never be quite sure if your next puff will be your last—the one that causes the balloon to burst.

Is there a way of blowing up balloons that will let you inflate them to their full size without breaking? And can you inflate those small balloons without hurting your cheeks? In this section one technique is suggested for overcoming these problems.

The Bicycle Pump Method

Pumps that are used to inflate bicycle tires can also be used to blow up balloons. One kind that is most useful is shaped like this.

Since this pump has a place for your feet to hold it down, it frees both your hands for pumping.

There are also different attachments that connect the pump to the stem of the tire. Many pumps have this arrangement.

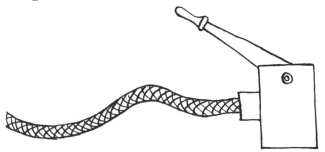

If it is working properly, a bicycle pump should push out the same amount of air with each pump. This is useful to know because you can count the number of pumps it takes to blow up a balloon until it breaks. Then, the next time you inflate the same-size balloon, you can stop pumping just a few pushes before you reach the balloon's breaking point.

The bicycle pump method will allow you to make comparisons among different kinds of balloons. For example, you will be able to figure out if sausage-shaped balloons hold more air than round ones. You will also be able to determine the different balloons' *maximum capacities*, or the greatest amount of air the various types of balloons can hold. This information will be useful when you are making the models and doing the experiments in this book.

Try blowing up various shapes and sizes of balloons. (Note that for all the projects in this book, the balloon dimensions are the size of the balloons when they are fully inflated.)

You will need:

> 1 bicycle pump
> 2 or 3 packages of assorted balloons: small (water bomb), large, round, oblong (airship), and narrow (sausage)
> 2 or 3 packages of 7-inch round balloons
> 1 package of 9-inch round balloons
> 1 package of 10-inch round balloons
> several very narrow balloons, approximately 36 inches long (optional)
> 1 dowel, 8 inches long and approximately ⅜ inch in diameter

1 empty ball-point pen tube
1 package of assorted rubber bands

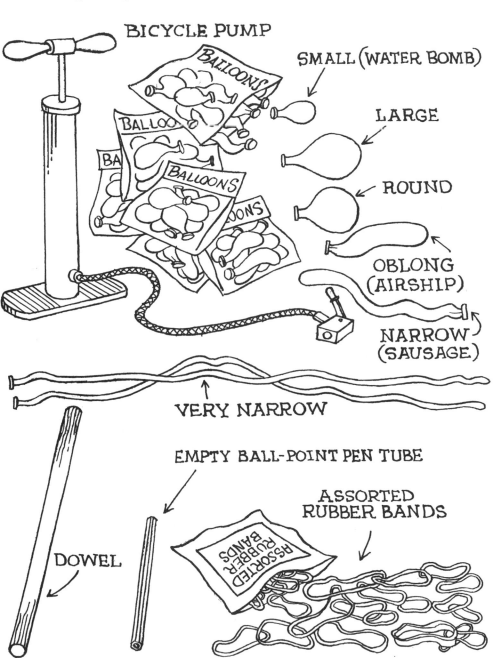

BICYCLE PUMP

SMALL (WATER BOMB)

LARGE

ROUND

OBLONG (AIRSHIP)

NARROW (SAUSAGE)

VERY NARROW

EMPTY BALL-POINT PEN TUBE

ASSORTED RUBBER BANDS

DOWEL

Step 1. Place the neck of the balloon directly onto the pump attachment.

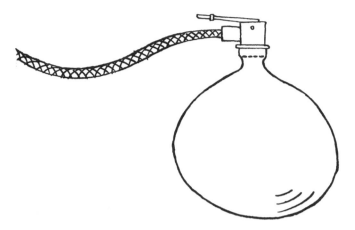

Step 2. Some smaller balloons may not fit easily around the pump attachment. To make an adapter, insert the outer tube of an empty ball-point pen into the hole of the attachment. Secure the balloons to the free end of the ball-point pen tube with a rubber band.

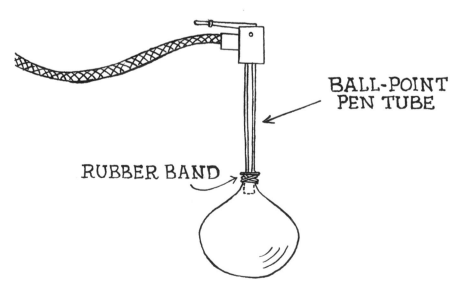

BALL-POINT
PEN TUBE

RUBBER BAND

Step 3. Have someone help you pump up the balloons. One person can hold the neck of the balloon on the pump attachment or ball-point pen adapter while the other person operates the pump.

Step 4. Practice pumping up a few balloons to their maximum size. Remember to bring the handle of the pump all the way up each time and then push it all the way down. This way the same amount of air will go into the balloon with each pump.

Experiments to Try

When you do the following experiments, don't forget to record your results. The information you gather will be helpful when you do other projects in this book.

Choose a balloon and count the number of pumps you need to blow it up until it breaks. Repeat with other balloons of the same type. Do you reach the same number of pumps, or almost the same number, each time?

Inflate a small, 5-inch round balloon and a long, 10-inch
sausage or airship balloon to its near-maximum
capacity. Which balloon holds more air?

Give a small round balloon and a short sausage balloon the
same number of pumps. How do they compare in
size? Does one look much bigger than the other?

Blow up a small round balloon to the breaking point.
Don't forget to count the pumps. Then blow up
another round balloon that is about twice the diameter of the first. Does it take twice as many
pumps of air to break the larger balloon?

If you can find narrow, 36-inch sausage balloons, compare
their capacity to wider sausage balloons. Which
type can hold more air?

Place one balloon inside another using the following technique: Slide one balloon onto a smooth dowel with
a rounded top. Hold down the neck of the first
balloon and slide a second balloon on top of it.

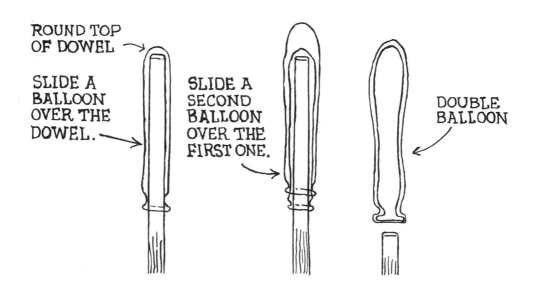

ROUND TOP
OF DOWEL

SLIDE A
BALLOON
OVER THE
DOWEL.

SLIDE A
SECOND
BALLOON
OVER THE
FIRST ONE.

DOUBLE
BALLOON

Now make a triple balloon by sliding a third balloon on top of the first two.

Remove the layered balloons from the dowel and attach them to the pump. (You might need someone to help you do this.) Does either the double or triple balloon hold more air before breaking than the single balloon?

What's Happening?

When you pump up the same kind of balloon to its maximum size, you should obtain consistent results. This does not mean that it will take exactly the same number of pumps each time to break a particular type of balloon, but you should obtain numbers within a range of 3 to 4 pumps.

Sometimes a balloon may burst long before it reaches maximum capacity. Some balloons have defects that cause them to break easily. Different manufacturers may make balloons of slightly different thicknesses. So if you are comparing two balloons of the same size and shape, you may not necessarily obtain the same results if the balloons come from different packages.

To help you make fair comparisons, try to secure the balloons to the adapter the same way each time. Also, try to make consistent pump strokes that go all the way up and down.

Generally, the larger the size of the balloon, the more air it will hold. As you would expect, large round balloons take many more pumps to break than small round ones.

Double-layering a balloon doesn't double its *capacity* (the amount of air it can hold). You can pump more air into a double balloon, however, compared to a single balloon of the same size and shape. But this is because the double balloon is stronger. You should have observed that the inflated surface of the double (and triple) balloon feels much harder than the surface of a single balloon does. This is because the air is pushing much harder against the stronger, layered balloon skins before they break.

In all of these experiments, you are comparing the maximum amount of air that you can squeeze into a balloon. When you first start pumping, you can see the balloon changing size. However, a point is reached when the balloon is still taking in more air but its size is no longer changing. The rubber skin of the balloon has reached the limit of its flexibility. At this point you can see and feel the skin of the balloon becoming much tighter. The air inside is pushing out harder because more of it is occupying the same space. This force will eventually become great enough to break the rubber skin. Small balloons have even less material to be stretched, so their breaking point is reached sooner.

There is one other important point to think about regarding the force of the air in a balloon. The air inside a large balloon does not necessarily act with a greater force than the air inside a small balloon. It is a combination of the amount of air and the space into which it is being squeezed that determines the force the air will exert inside the balloon. If you have a small balloon with lots of air squeezed into it, the force will be greater than the same amount of air in a large balloon, especially if the skin of the balloon is very strong. A bicycle inner tube is an example of this. The force of the air inside this small tube is strong enough to support the weight of a bicycle and a rider.

PROPULSION MODELS

If you let the air escape from a fully inflated balloon, the balloon will fly all over the room. The balloon is said to have *propulsion*. The air rushing to get out of the balloon pushes it in the opposite direction from the airflow. In this way the balloon acts like a miniature rocket.

The power obtained from balloons isn't very great, but it is enough to move small scale models. In this chapter you will learn how to construct models of a monorail, a car, a boat, a submarine, and a whirlaway. Most of the materials you will need are probably already around your house. You can have lots of fun making these models with very simple and inexpensive materials. Although you could obtain even more dramatic results with special equipment, working with simple materials is more challenging. You will become very familiar with properties of balloons, and you will also discover some of the scientific properties of gases of any kind, including air.

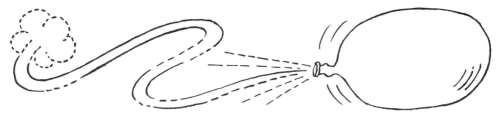

A Monorail

Have you or any of your friends ever taken a ride on a monorail? Perhaps you have seen a photograph of the famous monorail at Disney World. This form of transportation has only one rail for the train to travel on instead of two. The result is a faster, smoother ride.

Someday, rockets or jet engines on top of the train cars might provide even more speed and power. Although this may never actually happen, it is fun to play around with models to see how such a train might work.

Release an inflated balloon and watch it fly all around. It acts like a miniature, short-lived rocket. But rockets travel in a straight line. This is because the escaping gases are very carefully controlled and the rocket is well balanced. To make your balloons travel in a straight line you can attach them to a harness on a string. Depending on the type of harness and the kind of balloon used, you can make your balloons travel 16 to 60 feet. Your challenge is to determine the longest distance you can get a balloon to travel in this manner.

You will need:

> balloons of various sizes and shapes
> plastic tubing, several inches long by ⅜ or ½ inch
>   in diameter (available at hardware stores)
> 50 feet of thin string
> 3 empty ball-point pen tubes
> masking tape
> tape measure
> rubber band
> scissors
> bicycle pump
> hacksaw

Step 1. Find a large room or someplace outdoors and measure off a distance of at least 24 feet. (A longer distance would be even better.)

Step 2. Slide 2 ball-point pen tubes onto the piece of string. Tape the ball-point pen tubes together as shown.

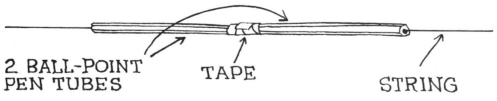

2 BALL-POINT PEN TUBES   TAPE   STRING

Step 3. Tie one end of the string to a chair or some other stationary object. Tie the other end of the string to another chair or object at a distance of about 24 feet. Make sure the string is stretched very tightly.

Step 4. Place 2 loops of masking tape under the 2 ballpoint pen tubes.

LOOP OF MASKING TAPE

MAKE THE LOOPS WITH THE STICKY SIDE OF THE TAPE FACING OUT.

Step 5. Pump up a balloon with the bicycle pump, filling the balloon almost to its maximum capacity. Hold tightly onto the neck of the balloon so that no air escapes, and attach the balloon to the 2 pieces of tape. The neck of the balloon should be parallel to the string.

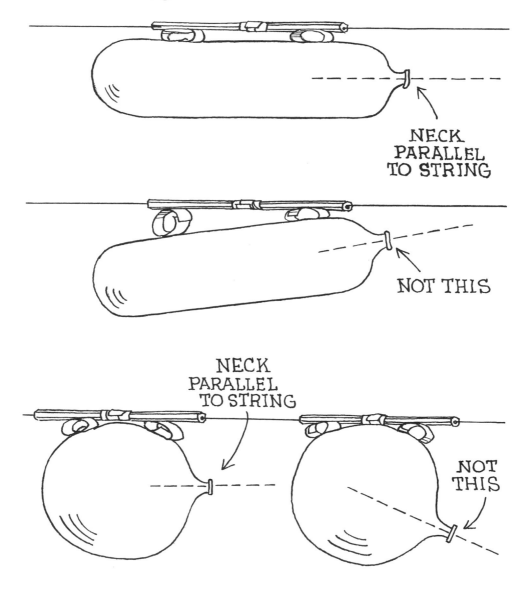

NECK PARALLEL TO STRING

NOT THIS

NECK PARALLEL TO STRING

NOT THIS

Step 6. Release the neck to let the air rush out. The balloon should propel itself along the string.

TROUBLESHOOTING

The way in which the balloon is attached to the ball-point pen tubes can make a big difference in how far it travels. Here are some hints to keep in mind.

Position the neck of the balloon parallel to the string. As the air rushes out of the balloon, the neck may end up pointing up or down instead of remaining parallel to the string. Check to see if the tape is sticking too tightly to the balloon. The tape should be just sticky enough to hold the inflated balloon, but it should still allow the balloon to pull off the tape as the balloon shrinks. Rub the sticky part of the tape on your clothes a little so that it will release the balloon as it should. Practice inflating, attaching, and releasing one kind of balloon until you can make it travel consistently along the string.

Experiments to Try
When you do the following experiments, be sure to record your results in a notebook as you go along. And remember to pull the pump handle all the way up and push it all the way down when inflating the balloons so you will pump the same amounts of air each time.

Inflate a small sausage balloon and a large sausage balloon to their maximum. Which one travels farther along the string?

Inflate a small sausage balloon and a large one with the same number of pumps of air. Which travels farther?

Inflate a small round balloon and a large round one to their maximum. Which one travels farther?

Inflate a small round balloon to about half its maximum size. Then inflate a large round balloon with the same number of pumps. Which one travels farther?

Inflate a sausage balloon and a round balloon with the same number of pumps. Which travels farther?

Which travels farther—a single balloon or a double balloon containing the same amount of air? (See page 16 for assembly directions.)

Fully inflate a 15-inch round balloon. How far does this balloon travel compared to all the others?

What's Happening?

Generally, the bigger the balloon, the farther it will travel along the string. So if you can attach a 15-inch round balloon to the ball-point pen tubes, you should be able to make it travel farther than the smaller round balloons.

On the other hand, the smallest balloons, such as those used for water bombs, and the very long, narrow type travel much faster than the big ones. You can observe how the air is pushed out of them very quickly. As soon as the air is expelled, however, the balloon stops, so that it travels only a short distance.

If the same amount of air is pumped into different-size balloons and then released, the smaller balloon goes farther. The smaller balloon will squeeze the air more forcefully, giving itself a bigger push.

When you double up a balloon by putting one inside another, the air will be pushed out faster compared to a single balloon of the same type. Therefore, the double balloon travels faster. In addition, the double balloon will travel a little farther than a single one containing the same number of pumps of air. Since you pumped the same amount of air into the double and single balloons, you would expect them to travel the same distance on the string. Why is there a difference?

Feel the surface of an inflated double balloon and compare it to the surface of an inflated single one. The double balloon feels much tighter. The air is pushing against the rubber surface with a greater force. In order to push air into the double balloon, you had to push a little harder, or exert a little more energy, with each pump than you did when filling up the single balloon.

Because the air in the double balloon is squeezed more tightly, it is at a greater pressure and has more energy.

This greater energy allows the balloon to travel slightly farther.

A Further Challenge
The large round balloons travel the farthest on the string. They can be made to travel even farther if the opening of the neck is made slightly smaller by the addition of a nozzle.

You can make a nozzle by attaching a small piece of plastic tubing to the balloon neck. You can also use a piece of ball-point pen tube.

With a hacksaw, cut a piece of plastic tubing about 1 inch long and secure it to the neck of the balloon with a rubber band.

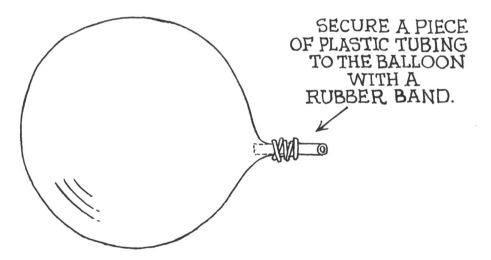

SECURE A PIECE OF PLASTIC TUBING TO THE BALLOON WITH A RUBBER BAND.

Inflate the balloon to its maximum capacity. How much farther does it travel along the string? If the diameter of the tube nozzle is too small, the balloon may not move at all. If the nozzle is too big, it also may not move. Experiment to see which size nozzle gives the best result. How much farther does the balloon travel with the best nozzle?

A Rocket Car

Another form of transportation that may change in the future is the automobile. Very fast-moving cars propelled by rocket engines would greatly reduce the time it takes to drive from one city to another. Already there are cars powered by jet or rocket engines that have been designed to break world speed records. Currently the world record is over 650 miles per hour.

You will discover some of the problems encountered by engineers who design rocket-engine cars when you make your own model of a balloon-propelled car.

You will need:

> balloons of various sizes and shapes, especially
> sausage- or airship-shape
> 1 empty paper half-gallon milk carton
> 2 pieces of coat-hanger wire or any sturdy wire,
> each approximately 8 inches long
> 4 thread spools or sewing bobbins, all the same
> size
> masking tape
> scissors
> tape measure
> bicycle pump

Step 1. Cut away a portion of the milk carton as shown.
The sides should be about 1 inch high. Leave the
back as is.

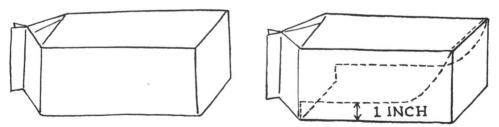

Step 2. Using scissors, carefully make a hole in the center
of the upright back section of the milk carton. The
hole should not be larger than ½ inch in diameter.

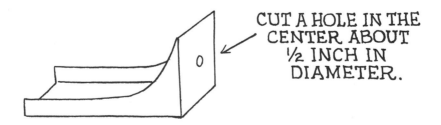

CUT A HOLE IN THE
CENTER ABOUT
½ INCH IN
DIAMETER.

Step 3. Tape the 2 pieces of wire onto the bottom of the milk carton. Press the masking tape as flat against the wires and carton as you can.

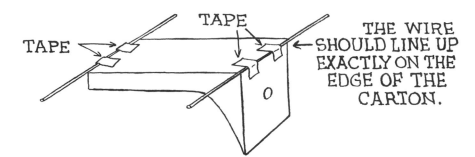

TAPE

TAPE

THE WIRE SHOULD LINE UP EXACTLY ON THE EDGE OF THE CARTON.

Step 4. Slide 1 spool or bobbin onto each end of the wires as shown. Wrap masking tape around the wires near the spools to prevent them from falling off the wires.

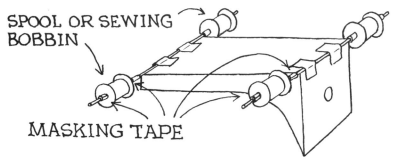

SPOOL OR SEWING BOBBIN

MASKING TAPE

Step 5. Place 2 loops of masking tape on the inside of the milk carton, about 6 inches apart. The balloon will be attached to these loops.

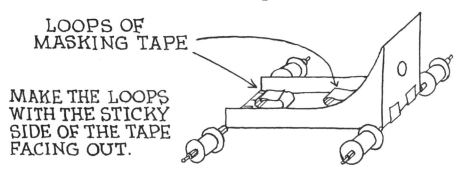

LOOPS OF MASKING TAPE

MAKE THE LOOPS WITH THE STICKY SIDE OF THE TAPE FACING OUT.

TRIAL RUNS

Test your model car by rolling it on the floor. Check to see if it rolls in a straight line. If it doesn't, examine the spools to see if they are on straight. Your car is now ready for some trial runs. Start off by using the larger sausage or airship balloons (those that become 24 to 30 inches long when inflated). Inflate the balloon and attach it to the milk carton by pressing it lightly onto the 2 loops of masking tape. The neck of the balloon should fit through the hole in the upright back section. To prevent air from escaping, hold onto the neck while you are positioning the balloon.

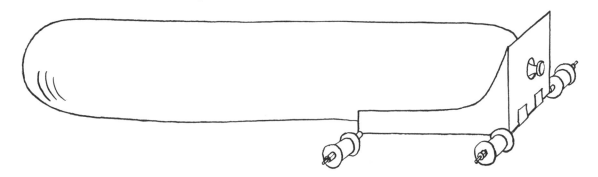

Place your car on a smooth floor in a space that is clear for at least 15 feet. If the wheels are working well and the balloon is fully inflated, your car should be propelled several feet. Can you make your model car travel up to 10 feet or even farther?

TROUBLESHOOTING

You may encounter some problems while launching your car. Here are some suggestions. Each time you are about to launch it, check to make sure the wheels are moving freely. Spin each wheel to make sure that none of them is rubbing against the tape.

The position of the neck of the balloon is also important.

Keep the neck parallel to the flat bed of the car. The hole in the upright back section should be just large enough to push the neck through. If it is too small, the air may come out too slowly. If it is too big, the balloon may fly off the car or jump around without pushing it in the right direction. (If the hole is too big, place small pieces of tape around the hole to make it smaller in size. Do this on both sides so that no sticky sections are showing.)

Before doing any experiments, practice your launching procedure. Use the same kind of balloon and try to solve any problems that come up.

Experiments to Try

Inflate each kind of balloon to its maximum size. Which kind propels the car the farthest? Which kind of balloon seems to move the car the fastest?

Inflate a 7- or 9-inch round balloon and a large sausage one with the same number of pumps. Which kind of balloon propels the car farther? Which kind goes faster?

Which goes farther, a large airship balloon or a small one? Which goes faster?

Place one balloon inside another. (For assembly directions, see page 16). Record your results with single, double, and triple balloons. Which combination goes farthest? Which goes fastest?

Repeat the previous experiment using the same number of pumps of air for each balloon. What are your results?

Inflate a large round balloon at least 15 inches in diameter. How does this balloon compare to all the others?

What's Happening?

No matter what kind of balloon you use, the model car does not travel as far as the monorail. Generally, larger balloons propel the car farther while smaller balloons make it travel faster over a very short distance. The largest round balloons may not move the car at all. The medium-size round balloons, about 7 to 9 inches in diameter, work the best for moving the car the farthest. Double or triple balloons move the car faster but not very far.

The results differ from the monorail for several reasons. The balloons in the model car have to overcome the weight of the car as well as fight against *friction*—the rubbing of the spools against the coat-hanger wire. This means that right from the start there has to be enough of a push by the escaping air to make the car move. Although a large round balloon has plenty of air, the escaping air doesn't have much force. On the other hand, smaller balloons and double or triple ones can make the model car start up easily. Because the air escapes quickly, however, the supply is soon gone. Although the car receives a big initial push, it slows down quickly and stops.

The larger sausage balloons work well. If they have a strong enough initial push to overcome the weight of the car, they can propel the car as forcefully as large round balloons. However, overall size is more important than shape.

To use the air in the balloon to the greatest advantage, you need a balloon that supplies a big enough push at the start but then doesn't continue to expel the air very fast. As you have found from your experiments, the medium-size round balloons fit this description best.

Matching the power of an engine to the job to be done is a problem engineers encounter often. A bigger and more powerful engine doesn't necessarily mean that a car will work better. Imagine placing a large truck engine in a small car. First, the car might fall apart from the weight and power of the engine. Second, the cost to operate such a car would be much greater, since a more powerful engine consumes more fuel. Furthermore, if you applied the full power of the engine to the wheels, you would probably end up spinning the wheels without the car going anywhere, as happens with regular cars when too much power is applied at once.

A Further Challenge

You know that a big push is needed to start your model car. A smaller push will keep the car moving. Can you design a balloon-powered car that will do this? By playing around with various combinations of large and small balloons, you may be able to make your car travel even farther.

For instance, you can create a platform for adding extra balloons to the car. Tape a piece of cardboard 12 inches by 6 inches to the bottom of the car as shown.

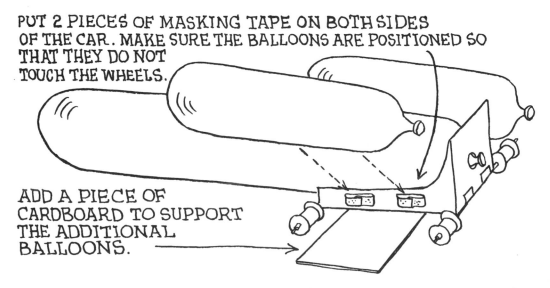

PUT 2 PIECES OF MASKING TAPE ON BOTH SIDES OF THE CAR. MAKE SURE THE BALLOONS ARE POSITIONED SO THAT THEY DO NOT TOUCH THE WHEELS.

ADD A PIECE OF CARDBOARD TO SUPPORT THE ADDITIONAL BALLOONS.

A Boat

A boat is a relatively slow means of transportation, so engineers are always trying to find ways to make them move faster. Today almost all boats have propellers driven by engines similar to those in cars and trucks. Experimental boats are being designed to see how fast they can travel. Some of these boats have engines in which a rocket or jet pushes against the air or water to move the boat.

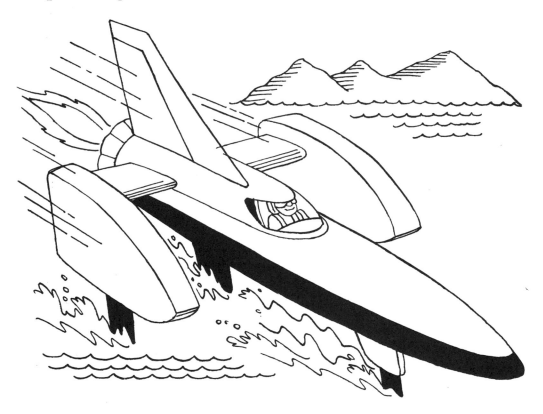

To design such boats, engineers first make small models and test them in a tank of water. You can invent your own rocket-powered boat by experimenting with a balloon-propelled model.

You will need:

> balloons of various sizes and shapes
> 1 empty paper half-gallon milk carton
> 1 empty ball-point pen tube
> masking tape or oil-based clay
> scissors
> rubber bands
> bicycle pump

Step 1. Cut away a portion of the milk carton as shown. The sides should be about 1 inch high. The back should be about 3 inches high.

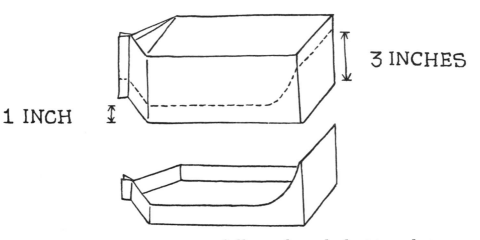

3 INCHES

1 INCH

Step 2. Using scissors, carefully make a hole ⅜ inch in diameter in the center of the upright back section of the carton.

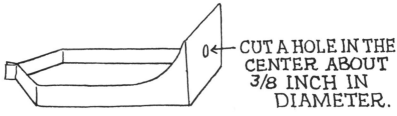

CUT A HOLE IN THE CENTER ABOUT 3/8 INCH IN DIAMETER.

MAKING A TEST TANK

Test your boat to make sure it doesn't take in water. You can use a bathtub filled with several inches of water or a large wading pool. You might also make your own test tank.

You will need:

> 2 pieces of wood, 6 inches wide and 8 to 10 feet long
> 2 pieces of wood, 8 inches wide and 16 inches long
> 12 nails, 2 inches long
> heavy plastic drop cloth, at least 30 inches wide and 10 feet long
> hammer
> bucket
> source of water

Step 1. Nail the four pieces of wood together as shown. The two long pieces of wood should butt each other at the bottom, forming a V shape.

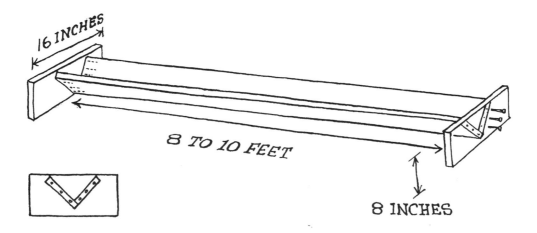

16 INCHES

8 TO 10 FEET

8 INCHES

Step 2. Line this tank with a heavy plastic drop cloth.
Make sure the cloth overlaps at the two ends.
Smooth the plastic so that there are no wrinkles.
Step 3. Fill the tank with water almost up to the top.

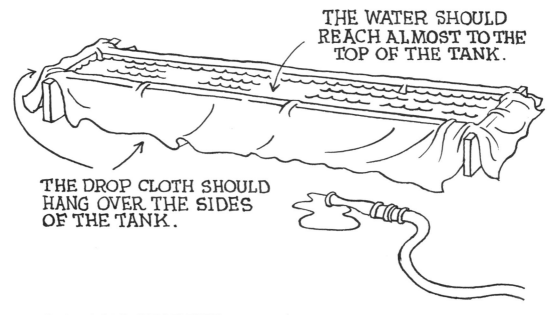

THE WATER SHOULD REACH ALMOST TO THE TOP OF THE TANK.

THE DROP CLOTH SHOULD HANG OVER THE SIDES OF THE TANK.

GETTING STARTED

Here is your challenge: Find out how far and how fast you can propel your milk-carton boat using an inflated balloon. Be sure to experiment with only one kind of balloon at a time so that you can make comparisons.

Using the same steps you did with the model car (see pages 29–30), practice attaching an inflated balloon to your boat and launching it in your tank.

You may find that with the neck of the balloon sticking straight out through the hole in the upright back section, the boat doesn't travel very far. This is because the air rushes out too quickly to keep the boat moving.

To get more power from the air, you need to slow it down. To do this, you can make a nozzle. Insert the ball-point pen tube into the neck of the balloon. Secure it with a rubber band. If the tube has a small hole on its side, place a piece of tape over it.

SECURE A BALL-POINT PEN TUBE WITH A RUBBER BAND.

Push the ball-point pen tube through the hole in the upright back section of the boat. Inflate the balloon through the ball-point pen tube and sit the boat on the water. Try placing the ball-point pen tube in different positions. Which position moves the boat the farthest?

TRY DIFFERENT POSITIONS FOR THE BALL-POINT PEN TUBE.

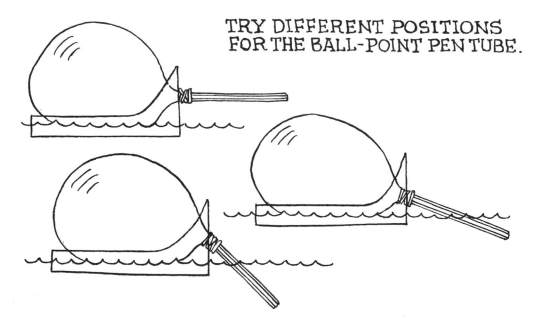

After you have figured out how to keep the balloon in the boat and how to make your model travel in a straight line, here are some more challenges.

Experiments to Try

Inflate a 7- to 9-inch round balloon and a 20-inch airship balloon with the same amount of air. Which travels farther?

Which travels farthest: a 9-, 12-, or 15-inch round balloon?

Does a double balloon move the boat any faster than a triple balloon? (See page 16 for assembly directions.)

Place masking tape or oil-base clay over one end of the ball-point pen tube. (Oil-base clay can be purchased at hobby shops, toy stores, and some large department stores having a craft section.) Then punch a small hole in the tape or clay to let the air escape. Does this smaller hole make any difference in your model's speed or distance?

What's Happening?

You may have been surprised at the short distances your boat moved, especially when compared to the monorail and car. Small water-bomb balloons or small sausage ones propel the boat quickly but only for a few feet. As before, the greater the volume of air or the bigger the balloon, the farther the boat travels. Even large round balloons, however, only move the boat a few feet.

The addition of a ball-point pen tube does move the boat farther. By placing a piece of masking tape on the end of the tube and then making a hole in it, you can better control the amount of air escaping from the balloon. A small hole lets out air slower than a bigger one. If the hole is just the right size, the boat will hardly move and can continue being propelled for a longer distance compared to the open tube.

The placement of the tube can also make a difference in

how far the boat moves. When the end of the tube is above water, the boat doesn't travel as far as when the tube releases the air below the water. However, there isn't much difference in the results with the two different pen positions in the water.

You can understand why this happens if you imagine how you lift yourself from a sofa. If the cushions on the sofa are very soft, it is harder to push yourself up than it is if the pillows are very firm. Firmer cushions offer more *resistance*, or push back more strongly. Water offers much more resistance than air. Therefore, the air escaping from the ball-point pen tube under the water can give a stronger push to the boat than the escaping air above the water pushing against just air.

Yet this same resistance that helps by pushing the boat also acts as a hindrance to keeping the boat moving. As you found out from your monorail experiments, a large balloon travels much farther on a string than when it sits in the milk-carton boat. And as you know from wading through water at the beach or in a swimming pool, it takes a great deal of effort to move your body against the water for any distance. One whole side of the milk carton sits in the water. This is a large surface to push through the water for the small force of air rushing out of the ball-point pen tube. Even if the force is increased by doubling or tripling a balloon, your model doesn't travel very far because the speeded-up boat still encounters the *drag* of the water on its bottom.

A Further Challenge

One way engineers have overcome the problem of drag is by designing boats that sit above the water. These boats have special fins that lift most of the boat out of the water when it reaches a certain speed.

To help your boat travel farther and faster you, too, can try to get part of your boat up out of the water. Cut 2 Styrofoam meat trays into sections about 4 inches wide and 6 inches long.

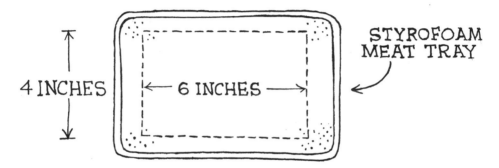

Tape one tray to each side of the milk carton. These "fins" should be large enough so that only the Styrofoam sits in the water. Reposition the ball-point pen tube so that its end is underwater.

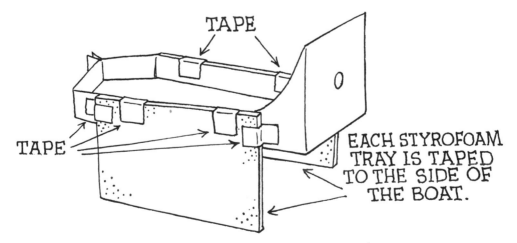

A SUBMARINE

Most fish move through the water by twisting their fins. Other sea creatures, such as the squid and the octopus, move by taking in and then ejecting water from their bodies like primitive, underwater rockets.

Someday there may be submarines that will move by taking in water and squirting it back out at high speeds. Balloons present an opportunity once again to investigate how this might happen. Instead of filling different balloons with air, you can fill them with water. The balloon will squeeze the water out when the neck of the balloon is released.

When placed in a pool of water, the balloon will dart around until all the water leaves it. However, not all balloons act alike. Here is a fun way to find out which balloons work the best.

You will need:

>   balloons of various sizes and shapes
>   bathtub, wading pool, or water tank (See pages
>   37–38 for assembly instructions.)

Experiments to Try

Place the neck of a round balloon on the end of a faucet.
Turn the faucet on slowly and fill the balloon with
water close to its maximum size. Then place the
balloon in a tank of water that is deep enough to
cover the entire balloon. Release the neck and
watch what happens. Repeat with different sizes of
round balloons and record your results.

Repeat the above experiment with sausage or airship
balloons.

Try doubling and tripling the balloons. (See page 16 for
assembly directions.) How does this affect their
movement?

What's Happening?

You should have discovered that the sausage balloons
travel much better through the water than the round
ones. In fact, the round ones will hardly move. Double
and triple sausage balloons will travel faster than a single
one. Why?

First, sausage balloons expel the water with a greater
force. You observed this already when you compared the
two different shapes as they propelled the car. Since double or triple balloons expel the water with a greater force,
they cause the balloons to move faster than a single one.

Second, the round balloon has a larger surface to push
through the water. To see this clearly, imagine cutting a

round balloon and a sausage balloon in half. Compare the two cross sections of these two types of balloons.

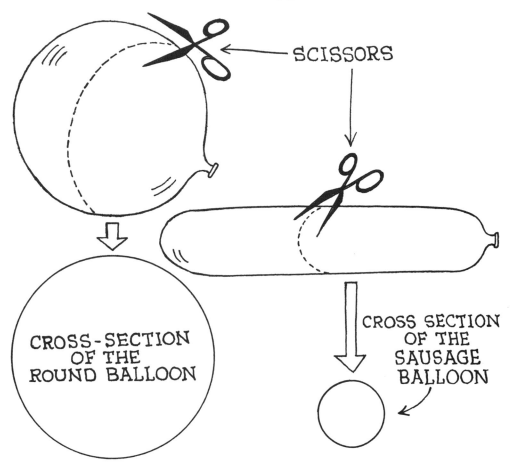

SCISSORS

CROSS-SECTION
OF THE
ROUND BALLOON

CROSS SECTION
OF THE
SAUSAGE
BALLOON

As you know, when you dive into water, you go much deeper if you keep your body straight instead of doing a belly flop. When an octopus crawls around on rocks, it has a large exposed surface; but when it wants to propel itself quickly through the water, its 8 tentacles stretch out behind its head, forming a smaller, streamlined cross section.

You will encounter this same principle in the following activity when you try to propel sealed balloons.

A Whirlaway

The ancient Greeks liked to invent amusing devices that were fun to watch in operation. Around 300 B.C., Hero of Alexandria made a device we call an *aeropile.* It looked like this.

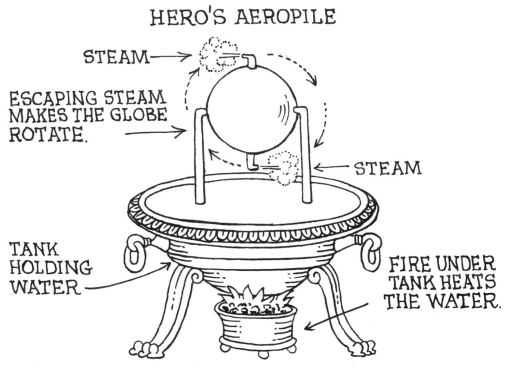

HERO'S AEROPILE

STEAM →

ESCAPING STEAM MAKES THE GLOBE ROTATE. →

STEAM

TANK HOLDING WATER →

FIRE UNDER TANK HEATS THE WATER.

Steam was produced in the bottom tank and was fed through pipes in the round section. As the steam escaped, it made the globe spin.

For a long time this contraption was looked upon as an amusing toy serving no practical purpose. Much later some inventors realized that the steam which made the globe move could be used to move even larger things. Eventually, steam was used to drive powerful engines in steamboats and locomotives.

Balloons can be made to spin like Hero's aeropile, but you don't need steam. Using only a flexible drinking straw, you can make a toy that will spin around in circles. Its movements can sometimes be humorous. As you play with this device, maybe you can think of some practical use for it.

You will need:

      round balloons of various sizes
      1 package of drinking straws with flexible ends
      3 or 4 rubber bands
      scissors

Step 1. Cut several flexible straws as shown.

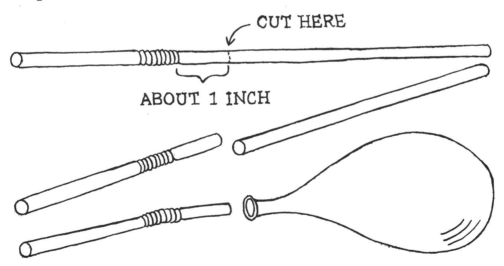

Step 2. Insert the piece of flexible straw into the neck of a round balloon and secure it with a rubber band. Do not wrap or tie the rubber band too tightly. This could crush the straw and prevent the air from escaping fast enough.

Step 3. Blow the balloon up to medium size. Quickly place a finger over the hole in the end of the straw. Put the balloon on the floor with the straw parallel to the floor and bent at about the angle shown.

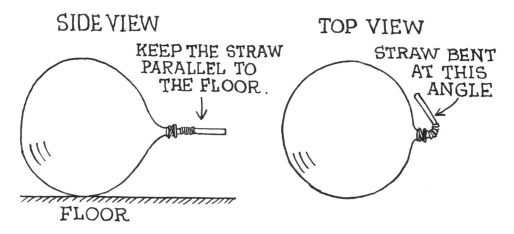

SIDE VIEW

KEEP THE STRAW
PARALLEL TO
THE FLOOR.

TOP VIEW

STRAW BENT
AT THIS
ANGLE

FLOOR

Step 4. Let go of the straw and watch what happens.

Experiments to Try
Bend the straw at different angles and observe how this affects the movement of the balloon.
Repeat the experiments with different sizes of round balloons as well as double and triple balloons. (See page 16 for assembly directions.)

What's Happening?
If the straw is bent toward the balloon and the air is escaping fast enough, your balloon should rotate. Observing the movement of the straw outlet relative to the floor, you should notice that it is not always parallel to the floor. Sometimes this outlet is higher above the floor or closer to it. Because of this, the direction of rotation is not always consistent. It may in fact change its direction of rotation.

This happens because the bottom of the balloon is not fixed to the floor. Any slight bump or piece of dirt can cause the air outlet to change position and thus make the balloon change its direction of rotation.

The angle at which you bend the straw determines the speed of rotation. When the angle is small, the balloon spins faster than it does when the angle is large.

In order to understand what is happening, we can compare it to another kind of situation. Suppose a person on ice skates is trying to move a very large, heavy ball in an ice skating rink. The bottom of the ball rests on a line.

TOP VIEW OF SKATER

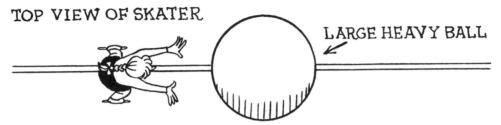

LARGE HEAVY BALL

The skater can push on the ball several different ways.

If she pushes in the same direction as the line, the ball moves forward along the line, and she moves backward along the line.

THE SKATER PUSHES THE BALL.

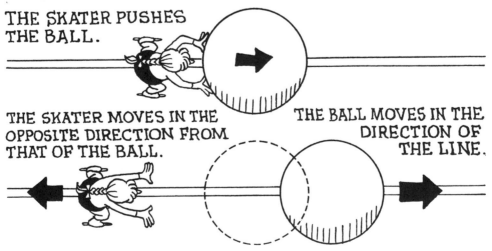

THE SKATER MOVES IN THE OPPOSITE DIRECTION FROM THAT OF THE BALL.

THE BALL MOVES IN THE DIRECTION OF THE LINE.

If she pushes at a large angle from the line, most of this force will go into rotating the ball. Some of it will cause the ball to move a little way away from the line, and she will move off at an angle.

THE SKATER PUSHES THE BALL AT A LARGE ANGLE FROM THE LINE.

THE SKATER MOVES SLIGHTLY AWAY FROM THE LINE.

THE BALL ROTATES BUT ALSO MOVES SLIGHTLY FROM THE LINE.

If she pushes at a slight angle, more of the force will go into moving the ball forward than in causing it to rotate.

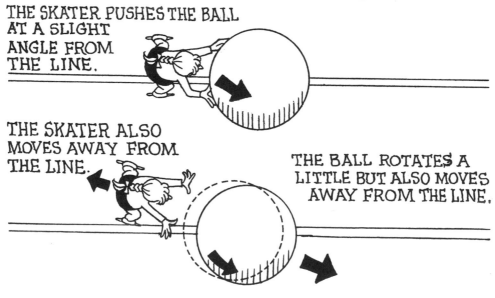

THE SKATER PUSHES THE BALL AT A SLIGHT ANGLE FROM THE LINE.

THE SKATER ALSO MOVES AWAY FROM THE LINE.

THE BALL ROTATES A LITTLE BUT ALSO MOVES AWAY FROM THE LINE.

The air escaping from a balloon pushes against the balloon as it is leaving. In the previous models the air escaped from the balloon along the same line as the balloon was being pushed, but in the opposite direction. The result was that the models went in a straight line. By using a bent piece of straw, you have changed the way the air pushes on the balloon as it leaves. Similar to the ice skater pushing on the ball, different angles of pushing cause the balloon to rotate at different speeds. Also, if it is pushed with a greater force, the balloon will spin faster. Since double and triple balloons expel air with a greater force than a single one, they will make the balloon rotate faster.

You may have noticed another curious effect. When most of the air is gone, the balloon rotates faster and faster. This happens because more and more energy is being given to the rotation of the balloon from the escaping air. This is similar to rotating a small merry-go-round in a playground. If you keep giving pushes to the merry-go-round as it is rotating, it will move faster and faster.

MEASURING THE FORCE OF AIR IN A BALLOON

You have discovered that some balloons propel your models with more force than others. Water bombs or narrow sausage types expel their air very quickly. A double balloon expels its air much faster than a single one. Does this mean that a water bomb balloon is more forceful than a 12-inch round balloon? Is a double balloon more forceful than a single one? Can one balloon be made to inflate another?

A Push Me–Pull You Toy

You can connect balloons of different types and have a pushing contest to see which balloon is more forceful. You may be surprised at the results.

You will need:

> balloons of various sizes and shapes
> 1 empty ball-point pen tube

1 empty plastic 2-liter soda bottle
rubber bands
pencil or dowel, ⅜ inch in diameter
knife
masking tape
bicycle pump

Step 1. Tape over the tiny hole in the side of the ball-point pen tube if there is one. Secure one kind of balloon to the tube using a rubber band. Inflate the balloon to one-half or three-quarters of its maximum size. Twist the neck so that the air cannot escape.

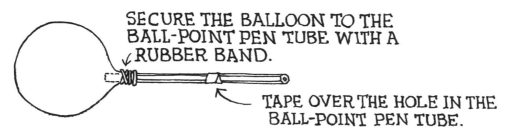

SECURE THE BALLOON TO THE BALL-POINT PEN TUBE WITH A RUBBER BAND.

TAPE OVER THE HOLE IN THE BALL-POINT PEN TUBE.

Step 2. Have someone hold the ball-point pen tube and the inflated balloon. Secure another kind of balloon on the other end of the inflated tube.

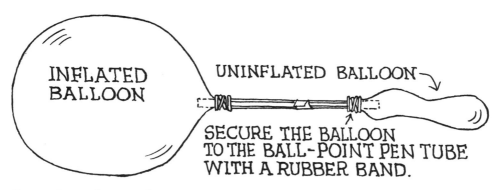

INFLATED BALLOON

UNINFLATED BALLOON

SECURE THE BALLOON TO THE BALL-POINT PEN TUBE WITH A RUBBER BAND.

Step 3. Release the neck of the inflated balloon and observe the result.

GETTING STARTED

If you have connected a water bomb to a large round balloon, the smaller balloon will push almost all its air into the larger one. If you squeeze the air from the large round balloon back into the water bomb, the smaller balloon will push the air right back again as soon as you stop squeezing the larger one!

As you practice using this toy, you may find it hard to squeeze the balloons with your hands to force the air back and forth. Placing the weaker balloon inside a plastic 2-liter soda bottle will help you do this more easily.

Cut the bottom off the soda bottle. Then, starting with an arrangement that has the stronger balloon inflated, slide the weaker balloon and part of the ball-point pen tube through the neck of the bottle.

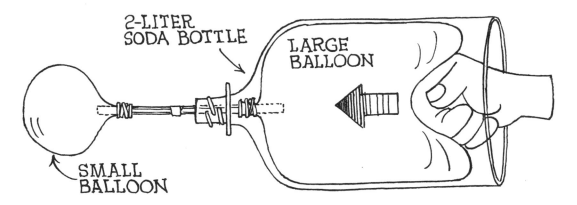

Releasing the neck of the stronger balloon will result in the other balloon becoming inflated until it reaches the sides of the bottle. Put your hand inside the bottle and push. You should be able to push the air out of the large balloon back into the small balloon. Taking your hand away will then result in the large balloon being inflated again.

Experiments to Try
Now try pairing different kinds of balloons.

Pair a double balloon with a single one. Will the double
    balloon inflate the single one?
Will a small sausage balloon blow up a larger one?
Will a triple round balloon blow up a double round bal-
    loon?
Which balloon will inflate any balloon at all that is con-
    nected to it?

What's Happening?
Generally, smaller balloons will blow up bigger balloons,
double balloons will blow up single balloons, and triple
balloons will blow up double balloons. And you have already discovered that it is more difficult to inflate very
small balloons.

The rubber skin of a small balloon is less flexible and
harder to stretch. Placing one balloon inside another
means that you have to stretch 2 or 3 balloons instead of
1. The result is that you have to put more energy into
squeezing air into these balloons because of the tighter or
thicker rubber skin. The air inside smaller and layered
balloons pushes with more force against the sides.

Making a Force-Measuring Device

So far your experiments have demonstrated that some balloons expel their air more quickly and forcefully than others. Using the push me–pull you toy, you were able to rank the balloons from strongest to weakest. When engineers or scientists work with models, they try to find ways of measuring such forces more directly and precisely.

Do you think you can design a device using inflated balloons that would measure the force of escaping air? This instrument would not have to be very complicated. Here is one way to make a force-measuring device from simple materials.

You will need:

> balloons of various sizes and shapes
> clear flexible plastic tubing, 2½ feet long by approximately ⅜ inch in diameter
> clear flexible plastic tubing, 6 feet long by approximately ⅜ inch in diameter (can be purchased at any hardware store)
> 1 No. 3 rubber stopper with 2 holes (can be purchased from a science supply house), or oil-base clay, or silicone cement
> 1 empty plastic 1- or 2-liter soda bottle
> yardstick or meter stick
> bucket (or other container) for water
> bicycle pump
> masking tape

GETTING STARTED

To carry out your measurements, you will have to seal up the bottle. This can be done in several ways.

Two-Hole Stopper

Place the stopper in the bottle and push the 2 pieces of tubing through the holes. Wetting the end of the tubing will help you slide it through the holes in the stopper. Your arrangement should look like this.

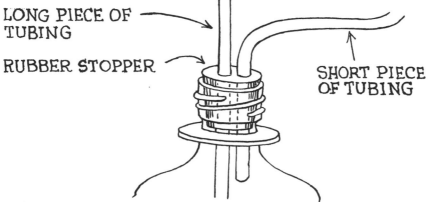

LONG PIECE OF TUBING

RUBBER STOPPER

SHORT PIECE OF TUBING

Oil-Base Clay

Pack a wad of oil-base clay around the 2 pieces of tubing and stuff it into the neck of the bottle. Fill the entire neck with the clay.

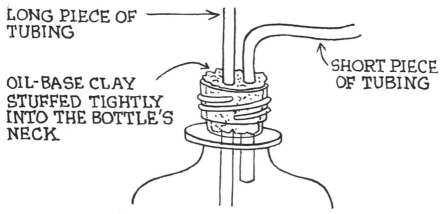

LONG PIECE OF TUBING

OIL-BASE CLAY STUFFED TIGHTLY INTO THE BOTTLE'S NECK

SHORT PIECE OF TUBING

Silicone Cement

Arrange the 2 pieces of tubing in the bottle, the same as above. Place some silicone cement in the neck of the bottle. Don't fill the entire neck with this sealant because it won't harden if it is too thick. Let it harden overnight. Add a little bit more cement the next day. Let it harden overnight once again.

To test any of the 3 types of seals, you will have to place the neck of the bottle underwater in a bucket. Fold one piece of tubing and hold it tightly so no air can escape. Blow into the other piece of tubing. If the seal is good, no air bubbles should be seen in the bucket of water. If there are air bubbles, repack the clay, add more silicone cement, or push the stopper down tighter.

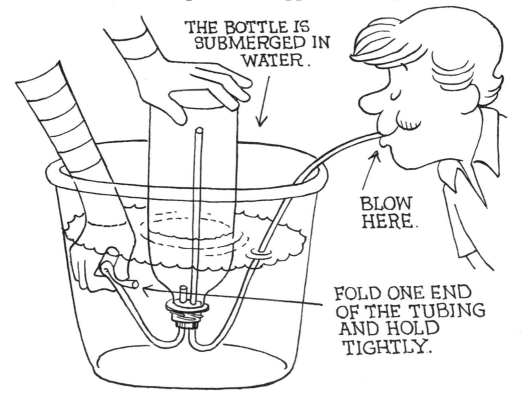

THE BOTTLE IS SUBMERGED IN WATER.

BLOW HERE.

FOLD ONE END OF THE TUBING AND HOLD TIGHTLY.

Step 1. Half fill the bottle with water. To do this, place the end of the shorter piece of tubing into a bucket of water and suck at the end of the other piece of tubing to start the water flowing. (To stop or reverse the flow, blow into the piece of tubing.)

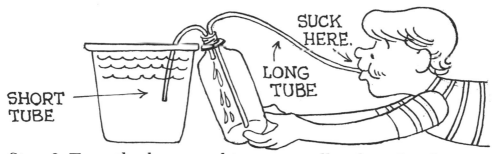

SHORT TUBE

SUCK HERE.

LONG TUBE

Step 2. Tape the longer tubing to a wall or board to keep it vertical. Tape a yardstick or meter stick alongside the piece of tubing.

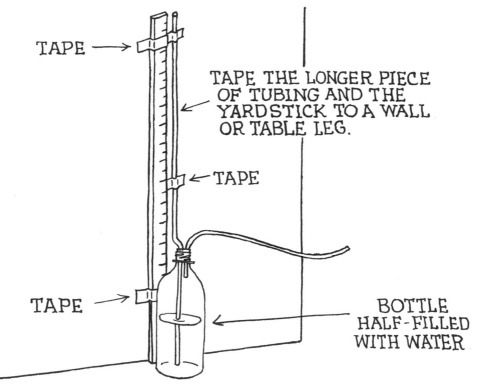

TAPE →

TAPE THE LONGER PIECE OF TUBING AND THE YARDSTICK TO A WALL OR TABLE LEG.

← TAPE

TAPE →

BOTTLE HALF-FILLED WITH WATER

Step 3. Inflate a balloon. Carefully wrap the neck around the end of the loose piece of tubing and hold it in place with your fingers. Make sure no air is escaping between the neck of the balloon and the tubing.

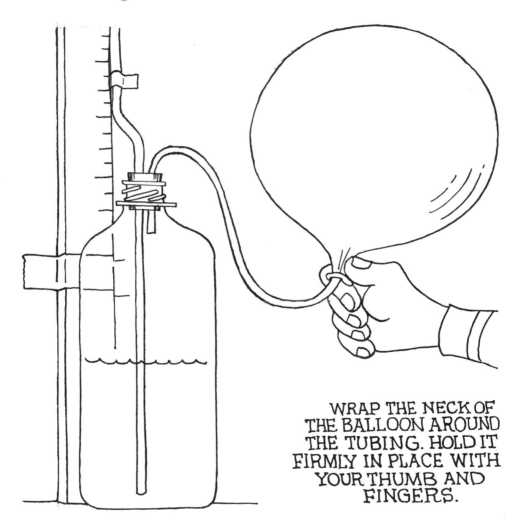

WRAP THE NECK OF THE BALLOON AROUND THE TUBING. HOLD IT FIRMLY IN PLACE WITH YOUR THUMB AND FINGERS.

If your arrangement is working correctly, water should rise up in the vertical piece of tubing when you release the air in the balloon.

Experiments to Try

Before you experiment with your force-measuring device, think about the results of the projects you have done so far. Try to predict which size and shape balloon will push the water the highest in the tube and which type will hardly push the water up at all. Write down your predictions in order, from the strongest to the weakest. Then begin testing to see if you are correct. Here are some other tests to try:

Place a single, then a double, and then a triple balloon on the bottle apparatus. How high does each type of balloon push up the water? Does the water rise 2 or 3 times as high as it did with a single inflated balloon?

Let air leak slowly out of the balloon into the room by holding the neck of the balloon loosely on the tube. How does the water level in the piece of vertical tubing change?

What happens to the water level in the tubing if any of the inflated balloons is squeezed while connected to the bottle?

What's Happening?

The results you obtain should be similar to those obtained with the push me–pull you toy. The greater the force in the balloon, the higher the water in the tube will rise. Therefore, the smaller, tighter water-bomb balloons push the water higher than the large round balloons. Smaller sausage balloons push the water higher than bigger sausage ones. Double or triple balloons also push the water higher than a single one.

As you gradually let air out of a large round balloon, the

height of the water decreases gradually in the spot where the difference between the highest and lowest point isn't very much. Letting air out of a small round balloon results in a quicker change in water level in the tubing, with about the same total change in the water level. This indicates that the air pushing out of either balloon is not pushing with the same force from the time it starts leaving the balloon until it is all gone.

Recall your results with the model car. A small balloon had enough force to move the car but didn't move it very far because it quickly lost its force and ran out of air. A large round balloon, fully inflated, starts with about the same force as the smaller one. It also makes the car move. However, it continues to push for a longer time with a larger force, and it also pushes for a longer total time since it has more air.

Scientists have given a special description to the force exerted by the air in the inflated balloons. They say the air is *exerting pressure*. Even though air is invisible and doesn't weigh very much, it still can act on its surroundings. When squeezed into small spaces, air can push back with a great deal of force. You saw this when you squeezed the inflated balloon in the last experiment. The tires on your bicycle or on a car are two examples of this. The heavy car or bike is held off the road by the air inside the tires. In the next chapter you will learn more about this property.

THE FORCE OF CONFINED AIR

In all the previous projects, the air was allowed to rush out of a balloon, with the result that the balloon was propelled forward. If you squeeze an inflated balloon, especially a smaller one, it will resist the force of your hand. In a way you could say that the balloon is pushing back. It might seem that this observation has no practical value. However, in recent years engineers and inventors have come up with ways to take advantage of air trapped inside containers. Inflatable furniture, inflatable buildings, and inflatable bags that lift up overturned trucks are among some examples of these recent inventions.

In this chapter you will be able to take advantage of the force of confined air in practical ways.

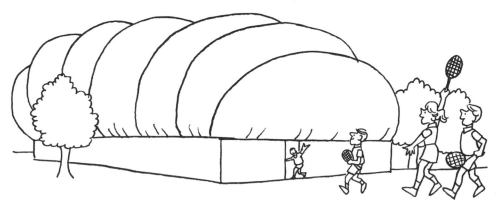

A Balloon Projectile _____

If you are wearing roller skates or ice skates and you push against a wall, you will move and the wall will stay where it is. This is because the wall is much heavier than you and is fixed to the ground. If two skaters of approximately the same weight push against each other, both will be repelled. When you push on an inflated, closed balloon and let it go, it will be propelled away from you. The size and shape of the balloon will determine the distance it can move.

It is an interesting challenge to see how far you can make a balloon travel. Making a balloon projectile is also an opportunity to learn about the force of confined air. A projectile is different from a rocket because the rocket is moved forward by the burning gases coming from its rear. A *projectile* is any object that is thrust into the air and continues to move through the air.

You will need:

> balloons of different sizes and shapes, including long, narrow ones that inflate up to 3 feet long (Not every variety store sells these kinds of balloons. Look in the Yellow Pages under Birthday Party Supplies or Novelty Items for suppliers.)
> several dowels, sticks, or broomsticks, approximately 12 inches long and from ¼ inch to about 1 inch in diameter
> measuring tape
> bicycle pump

Experiments to Try

Inflate several different kinds of balloons to their maximum size. Tie the neck of each so air cannot escape. How far can you throw each type of balloon? Measure the maximum distance each travels and record your results.

Hold onto a balloon with one hand. Push the balloon onto a pointed finger of the other hand as shown.

PUSH YOUR FINGER INTO THE NECK OF THE BALLOON GENTLY.

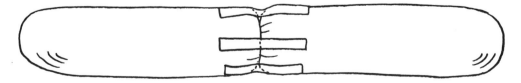

Release the balloon and see how far it travels. Measure and record the distances for different types of balloons. Practice your finger-launching technique to see if you can increase the distances.

If you were unable to obtain the very long, narrow balloons, you can try inflating and taping two of the larger sausage balloons together as shown.

PLACE 3 OR 4 PIECES OF TAPE AROUND THE ENDS.

Try launching this arrangement using the finger technique. Does this joined balloon travel a greater or lesser distance than a single balloon? Now try another approach. Use the balloon itself as the launcher and a dowel as the projectile. Hold the balloon in one hand. Place the dowel on top of the balloon. Gradually push the dowel down into the balloon a few inches.

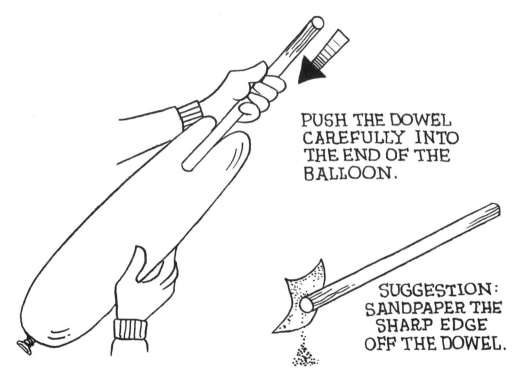

PUSH THE DOWEL CAREFULLY INTO THE END OF THE BALLOON.

SUGGESTION: SANDPAPER THE SHARP EDGE OFF THE DOWEL.

Then release the dowel suddenly. How far does the stick travel? Repeat this procedure several times to find the maximum distance the dowel can go without breaking the balloon when it is pushed farther and farther into it. Try the same procedure with other kinds of sticks, measuring how far they are projected.

SAFETY NOTE: Only attempt this activity in a clear area. Always point the dowel away from you and others.

What's Happening?

Whether a balloon is thrown with the hand or by using the finger-launching technique, some force is needed. You just can't throw the balloon without any force. The finger-launching technique allows you to focus this force, concentrating it on one small part of the balloon.

You should have discovered very quickly that the sausage balloon travels much farther than the round ones. Long, narrow balloons travel the farthest. When fully inflated, a 3-foot balloon can travel more than 20 feet using the finger-launching technique.

These results are similar to the ones you obtained from your experiments with balloons launched underwater. (See pages 44–45.) In that situation you found that the cross section of the balloon was a major factor in how well it moved through the water. Round balloons have a much larger cross section and therefore encounter much more resistance to air and water than long, narrow ones. The same is true here.

Have you ever tried to open an umbrella on a very windy day? When it is fully open, the umbrella can be pushed and pulled right out of your hands. If you point it into the wind, however, and open it just a little bit, you don't feel as much force. The wind blows past the umbrella without pushing on it.

If you tried launching sticks of different weights, you may have been surprised at how far even a heavy one could travel. As long as the stick is not too heavy, the air in the balloon will push it out.

This situation is an illustration of one of the famous laws of Isaac Newton. He proposed that for every action there is an equal and opposite reaction. You push on the balloon and the balloon pushes back on you with equal force.

You may have noticed that the sausage balloons travel straight for a few feet and then tend to turn sideways. This exposes a larger surface area to the air, which causes the balloon to slow down. Rockets have fin-like structures to keep them pointed straight ahead and help prevent this from happening.

Inflatable Furniture _____

You have seen that air trapped in a balloon can push back. Can you put this knowledge to practical use? Do you think confined air could push back with enough force to support your weight? This next challenge is fun as well as practical. Try to design a chair whose main material is air. This chair should be strong enough to support you or even a heavier adult.

You will need:

> 1 box of heavy-duty trash bags, 3 mils thick
> 1 cardboard box, 12 inches by 16 inches
> duct tape
> 1 package of plastic self-locking cable ties, 6 inches long (Both the duct tape and the ties may be purchased at hardware or electrical supply stores.)

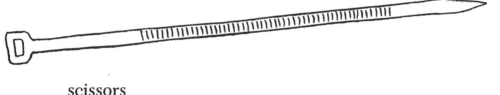

> scissors
> vacuum cleaner with an outlet that also expels air, or a bicycle pump

MAKING AN AIR CHAIR
Don't read the directions for making an inflatable chair just yet. First, try making your own designs using the materials listed. See how well you do. Then consult the directions for help.

Step 1. To inflate a trash bag, hold it open and move it around so that it captures some air. Then quickly close the bag. If you have the right kind of vacuum cleaner, you can use that instead. Hook up the hose to the exhaust end (where air is being blown out instead of sucked in). Insert the other end of the hose into a small opening in the bag and inflate the bag about three-quarters full. You can even use a bicycle pump, although this will take a long time.

Step 2. Seal the trash bag using duct tape or plastic ties. It helps to twist and fold over the end of the bag several times before applying duct tape or using the tie.

TWIST THE END OF THE BAG.

OVERLAP THE TWISTED END SEVERAL TIMES BEFORE SEALING IT WITH THE TIE OR DUCT TAPE.

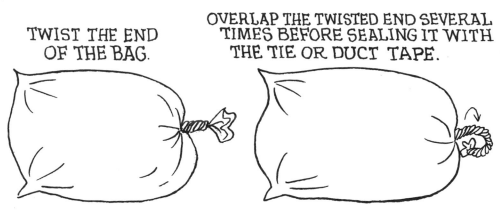

Step 3. Sit on your bag. Have someone help you so you don't roll over and fall on the floor. If no air is escaping, your bag chair should support you.

Step 4. To prevent the bag from rolling around and dumping you on the floor, stuff the bag into the cardboard box. The box will provide support and keep the bag in place. If the box is too high for your legs, cut one side of it lower.

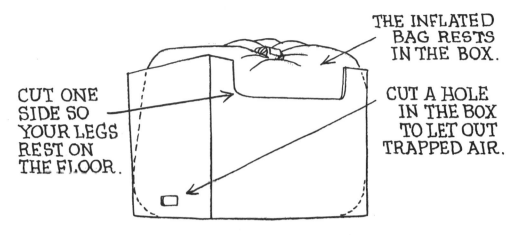

THE INFLATED BAG RESTS IN THE BOX.

CUT ONE SIDE SO YOUR LEGS REST ON THE FLOOR.

CUT A HOLE IN THE BOX TO LET OUT TRAPPED AIR.

Experiments to Try

Have people of different weights sit on the bag in the box.

How much weight can it support before it bursts?

Place 2 or 3 bags inside each other and inflate as before.

Does this make your air chair any stronger?

What's Happening?

When you sit on a single bag of air, it will support you as long as the plastic can withstand the increased air pressure. If the weight on the bag becomes too great, the increased air pressure can stretch the plastic to the point where it rips. By placing 2 or 3 bags inside each other, you make a stronger wall, which can better resist the increased air pressure.

When squeezed into small spaces, air, or gases of any kind, exert a great deal of pressure. Bicycle and truck tires filled with air support the weight of those vehicles. Automobile mechanics operate tools like drills or screwdrivers that are powered by compressed air.

Engineers have invented a very interesting use of air bags. They are used to lift up overturned trucks or airplanes. Special heavy-duty jacks are first placed under the truck and a small space opened up by operating these jacks. Then special bags made from heavy-duty rubber or plastic are inserted under the truck. Air compressors pump air into the bags, gradually inflating them so that the truck is slowly tilted back to its normal position.

MAKING AN AIR MATTRESS

Have you ever used an air mattress at the beach or while camping out? Air mattresses are usually very sturdy because they are made from heavy plastic. Now that you have made an inflatable chair, you can take up the challenge of making an inflatable mattress.

You will need:

        1 box of heavy-duty trash bags, 3 mils thick
        1 board, approximately 14 inches wide and 3 feet
            long
        duct tape
        1 package of plastic self-locking cable ties, 6 inches
            long
        scissors
        vacuum cleaner with an outlet that also expels air,
            or a bicycle pump

Step 1. Place 2 bags on a flat surface with the 2 open ends facing each other. Slide one bag inside the opening of the other a distance of about 6 inches.

ONE BAG OVERLAPS THE OTHER ABOUT 6 INCHES.

Step 2. Carefully place duct tape on the overlapping edge. The tape should go around both sides of the bags. Press down firmly to make the tape stick well.

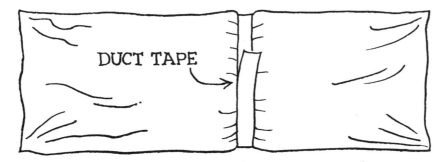

DUCT TAPE

Step 3. Repeat Steps 1 and 2, enclosing the first set of bags. This will give you a double-layered bag.

Step 4. Cut a small hole in one sealed corner through the two bags. Using a vacuum cleaner or the bicycle pump, inflate the bags until they are half filled. Then twist the end near the inflation hole into several overlapping layers and seal it with duct tape or plastic ties.

Experiments to Try
Your mattress is ready for testing.

Place the bags on the floor and carefully lie down on
them. If there are no leaks, your air mattress
should support you.

Place the board on top of the bags. Gradually add more
and more weight on top of the board. Books, a
bucket of sand, or other heavy objects can be
placed on the board until the bags break. You may
be surprised at how much weight it holds.

What's Happening?
When you sit on the inflated chair, all your weight is concentrated on a small area. When you lie down on the air
mattress, however, your weight is spread out over a much
larger area.

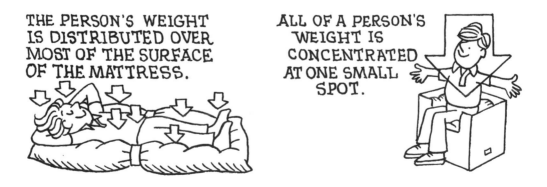

THE PERSON'S WEIGHT
IS DISTRIBUTED OVER
MOST OF THE SURFACE
OF THE MATTRESS.

ALL OF A PERSON'S
WEIGHT IS
CONCENTRATED
AT ONE SMALL
SPOT.

The mattress is less likely to break from a heavy weight than the chair because each part of the mattress is supporting only a small portion of the overall weight.

MAKING AN AIR-BAG PLATFORM

To take another look at pressure and get a better understanding of how it works, get together with some friends and try making an air-bag platform.

You will need:

> 1 piece of wood, 8 to 10 inches wide and 6 feet long
> 1 box of zipper-lock bags, 1-gallon size
> 1 box of zipper-lock bags, sandwich size
> drinking straws

Step 1. Close a gallon-size plastic bag by pressing down firmly on the zipper lock. Leave a small opening in one corner, just enough for a drinking straw to fit through. Blow into the straw until the bag is almost full. Remove the straw and close the small open section completely.

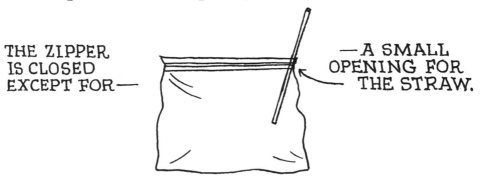

THE ZIPPER IS CLOSED EXCEPT FOR—

—A SMALL OPENING FOR THE STRAW.

Step 2. Inflate 7 or 8 gallon-size bags in this manner. Place them on the floor next to each other. Place the piece of wood on top of the bags.

Experiments to Try
Now have several of your friends stand on top of the board. Someone should remain off the board to help support the others, since the board will be unsteady.

SAFETY NOTE: Do not place any fingers or feet under the board to steady it. If the bags break suddenly, someone could be hurt.

Have your friends step off the plank and remove one bag. They should then step carefully back on the board. Do the remaining bags still support them?
Keep the number of persons constant and keep taking away bags one at a time until the remainder pop under the weight. What is the minimum number of bags that will support your friends?

Repeat these experiments with 8 to 10 sandwich-size bags. What is the minimum number of smaller bags that will support the same number of people as before?

What's Happening?

As you remove bags from under the board, the result is that each remaining bag is supporting more and more weight. Imagine a situation where 5 people weigh 100 pounds apiece. Their total weight is 500 pounds. If they are standing on 10 bags, each bag is supporting 50 pounds. If they are standing on 5 bags, each bag is supporting 100 pounds. If only 2 bags are under the board, each of the bags would have to support 250 pounds. There is a significant difference between 50 and 250 pounds. The plastic in the bags reaches a point where it can no longer support such great pressure and it breaks.

Smaller bags break sooner because there is a smaller area supporting the board compared to larger bags. A smaller area supporting the same weight is under greater pressure.

Scientists think about pressure in terms of a ratio of a weight or force acting over a certain-size area. A heavy force over a small area results in a high pressure. A small force over a large area results in a low pressure.

Recall your results with balloons in the previous sections, especially the push me–pull you toy and the force-measuring device. Small balloons blow up large round balloons and also push the water higher up the tubing. A lot of air squeezed into a small balloon means that the air pressure in that balloon is high. The same amount of air put into a large balloon results in a lower air pressure.

EXPERIMENTING WITH OTHER PROPERTIES OF BALLOONS

The projects in this book have given you the opportunity to learn about only a few of the properties of balloons as well as some of the physical properties of air. There are many other questions you could think about. For example, you know that helium gas will make a balloon float in the air. How many balloons do you think it would take to lift you off the ground? How many ordinary balloons would you need to keep yourself afloat in water?

Try drawing different pictures on your balloons and see how they change as air is added.

How do balloons change when placed in a cold refrigerator or a warm oven? How does a balloon shape change when it is filled with water instead of air? Can balloons be used to detect sounds?

You can design your own experiments to answer these questions. Can you think of more questions? Use the experience you have gained through doing the projects in this book to continue your explorations.